CONTENTS

Abbreviations **km** stands for kilometres • **m** stands for metres • **ft** stands for feet • **km/h** stands for kilometres per hour • **mph** stands for miles per hour • **°C** stands for degrees Centigrade • **°F** stands for degrees Fahrenheit

Boom!

You're on a high mountain. Suddenly, the ground starts to rumble and shake. There's a hissing noise. Then... BANG! A massive explosion blows the top of the mountain apart. Run for your life!

Deep inside, the Earth is made up of hot, molten rock, called **magma**. Volcanoes are places where the magma bubbles up and **erupts** through the Earth's surface. Once magma is out of the ground, we call it lava.

As well as lava, volcanoes hurl out massive solid rocks, burning ash, and deadly poison gas.

Volcanologists are scientists who study volcanoes. Here's one wearing a heatproof suit to watch Mount Etna erupting in Italy.

Active or not?

Volcanoes don't all erupt all the time. Some, known as active volcanoes, erupt regularly. Dormant volcanoes are resting, but may erupt again. Volcanoes that have stopped erupting for good are called extinct.

magma molten (melted) rock from inside the Earth

EXTREME!

Volcano's Edge

Danger on the Brink of Disaster

Anna Claybourne

A&

Safety advice
Visiting and studying volcanoes can be extremely dangerous. Only go close to a volcano, lava flow, or volcanic water feature if you are with an official organised tour or are using a well-marked, popular tourist route that is open to the public.

Produced for A & C Black by

Monkey Puzzle Media Ltd
48 York Avenue
Hove BN3 1JD, UK

Published by A & C Black Publishers Limited
36 Soho Square, London W1D 3QY

Paperback published 2010
First published 2009
Copyright © 2009 A & C Black Publishers Limited

ISBN 978-1-4081-1257-1 (hardback)
ISBN 978-1-4081-1994-5 (paperback)

The right of Anna Claybourne to be identified as the author of this Work has been asserted by her in accordance with the Copyright, Designs and Patents Act 1988.

A CIP catalogue record for this book is available from the British Library.

Editor: Susie Brooks
Design: Mayer Media Ltd
Picture research: Lynda Lines
Series consultants: Jane Turner and James de Winter

This book is produced using paper that is made from wood grown in managed, sustainable forests. It is natural, renewable and recyclable. The logging and manufacturing processes conform to the environmental regulations of the country of origin.

Printed in Malaysia by Tien Wah Press (Pte.) Ltd

Picture acknowledgements
Alamy pp. 4–5 (Greg Vaughn), 10–11 (David Sanger Photography), 20 (Gary Cook), 22 right (Interfoto Pressebildagentur), 24–25 (Jon Arnold Images Ltd), 28 (Jon Arnold Images Ltd); Corbis pp. 6–7 (Roger Ressmeyer), 8 (José F Poblete), 9 (DW Peterson), 12, 12–13 (Jacques Langevin), 14–15 (Benjamin Lowy), 16–17 (Roger Ressmeyer), 18 (Jay Dickman), 22 left (Bettmann), 23 (Danny Lehman); Getty Images pp. 6 bottom (Adastra), 24 left (AFP), 26 (Philippe Bourseiller); iStockphoto p. 19 (Sascha Burkard); PA Photos p. 15 top (AP); Rex Features pp. 10 (IBL), 16 (Roger-Viollet), 28–29 (Sipa Press); Science Photo Library pp. 1 (Jeremy Bishop), 4 top (Jeremy Bishop), 21 (George Steinmetz), 27 (Simon Terrey).

The front cover shows people at the edge of the crater of Mount Etna, a volcano in Sicily, Italy (Getty Images/DEA Picture Library).

Every effort has been made to contact copyright holders of material reproduced in this book. Any omissions will be rectified in subsequent printings if notice is given to the publishers.

Red-hot lava splatters from Kilauea volcano in Hawaii.

Look out for flying ash, smoke and solid rocks.

Boom!

Lava shoots out.

Runny lava flows down the mountain.

Hot magma comes from under the ground.

erupt to burst out suddenly

Look out – lava!

There's glowing, sizzling, liquid molten rock flowing towards your feet. It's horribly hot, like flames. You need to get out of the way or you'll be burned to a crisp.

Lava usually trickles quite slowly – but be careful. If you get trapped between two **lava flows**, they could close in on you. Stay away from bushes and trees too – plants sizzle, crackle and explode when lava flows over them.

Like all liquid, lava flows downhill. You can often avoid it by running to higher ground, such as a mountain ridge.

Lava cools into hard black rock.

Sometimes, lava plunges into the sea. It makes the water boil, hiss and steam.

Sizzle

lava flow   a trickle or river of lava

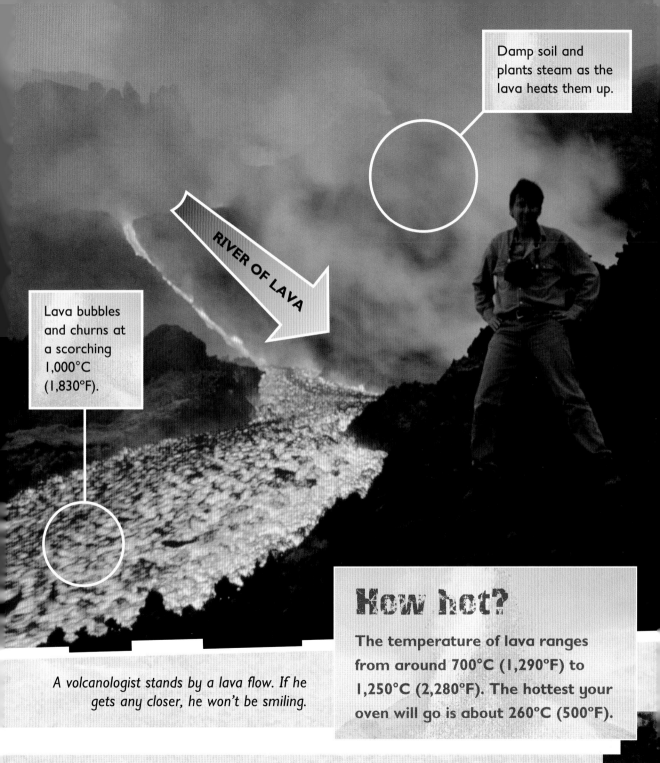

Damp soil and plants steam as the lava heats them up.

RIVER OF LAVA

Lava bubbles and churns at a scorching 1,000°C (1,830°F).

A volcanologist stands by a lava flow. If he gets any closer, he won't be smiling.

How hot?

The temperature of lava ranges from around 700°C (1,290°F) to 1,250°C (2,280°F). The hottest your oven will go is about 260°C (500°F).

Cool it!

You can actually walk on top of lava without your feet turning to toast. But only when it's cooled and hardened into solid rock.

A big lava flow is hottest in the middle and cooler on top, near the air. Sometimes, the top hardens first. This makes a **lava tube**, with a solid "roof" over a runny lava river — a bit like the thick skin on custard.

As lava cools, it sets in weird shapes. You can see patterns in the rock, such as lumps and bumps, spikes, sheets, wrinkles or rope-like strands.

Pahoehoe-type lava lies in wrinkles on the Galapagos Islands in the Pacific Ocean.

Lava lumps

Volcanoes such as Kilauea, in Hawaii, produce two main types of lava:
pahoehoe = wrinkly, ropy lava
aa = spiky, jagged lava.

lava tube a crust of cooled lava covering a lava flow

Volcanologist DW Peterson stands on a lava tube on Mount Kilauea, Hawaii.

A long pole can test the depth of the lava tube.

Is the tube strong enough to take a person's weight?

Cooled pahoehoe lava

Hot, runny lava

Don't step here!

Rivers of rock

So you think a lava flow's scary? Wait till you see a **pyroclastic flow** – a rushing, thundering mass of scorching hot gas, ash and rock.

In a pyroclastic flow, hot gas, ash and rock tumble and splash down a volcano's slopes. If they land on you, you're in big trouble.

In 1991, two volcanologists and forty-one tourists and journalists were climbing Mount Unzen, a volcano in Japan. A sudden pyroclastic flow caught up with them. No one survived.

In 79 BC, people were trapped and killed by pyroclastic flows from Mount Vesuvius, Italy. Their bodies rotted away, leaving human-shaped hollows of ash that have been filled with plaster to make these casts.

Ash hardened on the bodies before they rotted away.

Don't stand here!

pyroclastic flow   a fast-flowing river of hot volcanic ash, rocks and gas

Don't bother running

You can't outrun pyroclastic flows. They zoom along at speeds of up to 200 kilometres per hour (125 miles per hour).

A pyroclastic flow thunders from the Montserrat volcano in the Caribbean.

Flow travels this way, at 200 km/h (125 mph).

It's up to 1,000°C (1,830°F) in here.

Your only chance of escape is to sidestep the flow.

Mudflow mayhem

When volcanoes erupt, mud is one of the biggest killers. Mud can drown whole towns – even if they lie far away.

Volcanoes don't erupt mud. It forms when volcanic ash and dust mix with water. The water can come from rain or rivers, or from snow on the volcano melting in the heat. Rivers of mud are called mudflows, or **lahars**.

In 1985, the Nevado del Ruiz volcano in Colombia released a deadly mudflow. It swamped the town of Armero, 70 kilometres (45 miles) from the mountaintop. If the residents had known it was coming, they could have escaped. But tragically, more than 23,000 people died.

Mudflows

Mudflows

This photograph of mudflows from Mount Pinatubo in the Philippines was taken from space.

lahar a flow of mud down a volcano

People could have escaped by walking up here.

Cars, people and animals were trapped under the mud.

The fast-moving mud smashed up buildings.

This is all that was left of Armero, soon after the 1985 mudflow disaster.

Mudwatch

Today, space **satellites** can spot mudflows in advance. They send back pictures and information so that scientists can warn people to get away.

satellite a machine that is sent into space to collect and send back information

13

Tsunami terror

Will you be safe from a volcano if it's on a distant island? No! Lava and mudflows can't reach you – but volcanoes have another deadly weapon... the tsunami.

Tsunamis are huge, powerful waves of water that form when the sea moves suddenly. A volcano can make this happen, by hurling rock and ash into the water. Giant ripples spread out across the ocean, becoming enormous **breakers** when they hit the land.

In 1883, a volcano called Krakatau, in Indonesia, blew up with a mighty bang. A chunk of the mountain landed in the sea. It set off tsunamis that killed 36,000 people.

The city of Banda Aceh, Indonesia, was smashed up by a massive tsunami in 2004.

Tsunami waves towered over buildings.

The power of the water smashed up buildings.

tsunami a giant wave, or series of waves, forming a huge wall of water

The 2004 tsunami hit many countries including Thailand, where a tourist snapped a photo of this huge wave crashing ashore.

The force of the waves swept people, cars and boats far inland.

Giant waves

Some tsunamis have measured 500 metres (1,600 feet) high! The Krakatau tsunamis rose to about 30–40 metres (100–120 feet).

breaker a large, white-topped wave that is breaking onto the shore

Deadly gas

Burp! Belch! Hisssss! CHUFF-CHUFF-CHUFF-CHUFF-CHUFF! Volcanoes can make some very strange noises. Besides lava, rocks and ash, they often release gases.

Volcanic gases are brewed up deep inside a volcano. They can burst out during eruptions, or shoot or ooze from cracks on a volcano's sides, known as **fumaroles**.

Gas from eruptions can be deadly. In 1902, Mount Pelée on the island of Martinique spewed burning volcanic gas, mixed with ash and dust, onto the town of Saint-Pierre. It killed 28,000 people.

The killer gas eruption of Mount Pelée was caught on camera in 1902.

Stinker!

Hydrogen sulphide is a common volcanic gas. It smells like rotten eggs.

fumarole a crack or hole in the ground that gives out steam and gases

Gas mask stops the volcanologist from breathing in deadly gas.

A volcanologist collects a sample of volcanic gas from a fumarole.

Steam rises from heated underground water.

Stinky gas is trapped in a tube.

This equipment collects a pure sample of the gas.

A tripod holds the delicate gear steady.

Water features

When exploring volcano areas, watch out for bubbling pools. If you fall in, you could be boiled alive! The hot rock under a volcano can create natural hot springs, pools, and fountains. Some are too hot to touch – but others make a perfect bath.

Water often collects underground. When volcanic rocks heat it up, the water can boil, bubble, and shoot to the surface out of cracks. A jet of hot water like this is called a **geyser**. Iceland has lots of them, and so does Yellowstone National Park in the USA.

Tourists float in water from hot springs near the Arenal volcano in Costa Rica.

Monkey bath

On the Shiga Kogen volcano in Japan, wild macaque monkeys sit in the hot springs to keep warm.

spring a place where water flows from the ground

A crowd watches Old Faithful geyser in Yellowstone National Park, USA.

Water spurts up to 50 m (160 ft) into the air.

Whoosh!

The water shoots from a hole in the ground.

Erupted water sinks back down underground.

Underground heat boils the water before the geyser explodes again.

geyser a jet of hot water or steam spurting up from the ground

The volcano's edge

Imagine you're scrambling up a volcano's steep, cone-shaped slopes. At last you reach the top. But this isn't a pointed mountain peak. You're standing on the rim of a huge, bowl-shaped crater – the volcano's edge itself.

Steep, almost vertical sides

Cooled lava and ash

crater the bowl-shaped opening of a volcano

Tourists creep to the edge of the crater of Villarrica, a volcano in Chile.

Scientists stand near the crater at the top of Erebus, a volcano in Antarctica.

Inside a volcano, a long tube called a **vent** leads deep into the Earth. Hot, runny magma shoots up the vent when a volcano erupts. At the top, the vent opens out, forming a wide crater.

On some volcanoes, tourists can climb right to the top to see the crater. But they need to watch their step – it wouldn't be fun to fall in!

Weird water

Some craters fill up with rain, making a lake. Volcanic gases can give crater lakes a weird greenish colour.

vent the tube that leads from inside a volcano to its surface

Volcanoes from nowhere

You don't have to be near a volcano to see an eruption. In fact, volcanoes can appear from nowhere... out of the blue... maybe even right under your feet!

The Paricutin volcano erupts for the very first time.

I YEAR LATER

Changes or movements in the Earth's **crust** can create a new volcano.

Rock has built up on the mountainsides.

In 1943, Mexican farmer Dionisio Pulido was working in a cornfield when he noticed smoke, ash and rock pouring from a crack in the ground. He was watching the birth of a brand-new volcano – Paricutin.

A year later, the volcano is still erupting and has formed a cone-shaped hill.

crust the layer of hard rock that forms the Earth's surface

Volcanoes at sea

Volcanoes erupt from the seabed and break through the surface to make new islands. Surtsey, a small island near Iceland, formed in this way in 1963.

65 YEARS LATER

Mount Paricutin

The rest of this church is buried.

Hardened lava

Paricutin kept erupting for nine years. With every blast, more lava piled up around the vent. Eventually Paricutin grew into a cone-shaped hill, 424 metres (1,391 feet) high.

This is Mount Paricutin today, behind a town that it has buried in lava.

Living dangerously

Erm, don't build your house there! Around the world, millions of people live right next to deadly volcanoes. What are they thinking?

In 2006, people living near Mayon volcano in the Philippines left their homes after volcanologists warned of an eruption.

In fact, volcanoes aren't all bad news. Volcanic ash from eruptions makes soil rich and **fertile**, ideal for growing crops. So most volcanoes have farms and towns around them.

Many people live close to volcanoes because they have to. In Japan, for example, there are a lot of volcanoes and not much flat land for building on.

fertile full of things called nutrients, which help crops to grow

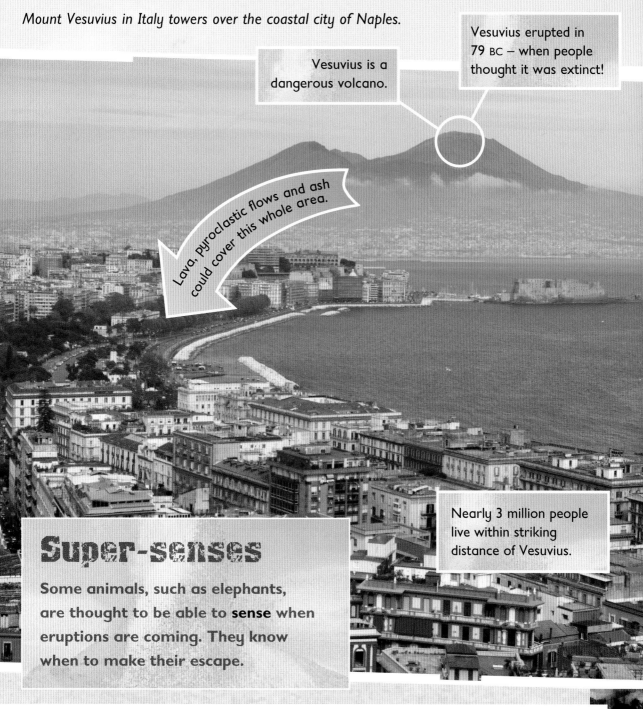

Mount Vesuvius in Italy towers over the coastal city of Naples.

Vesuvius is a dangerous volcano.

Vesuvius erupted in 79 BC – when people thought it was extinct!

Lava, pyroclastic flows and ash could cover this whole area.

Nearly 3 million people live within striking distance of Vesuvius.

Super-senses

Some animals, such as elephants, are thought to be able to **sense** when eruptions are coming. They know when to make their escape.

sense to detect something using natural senses, such as hearing

Supervolcano!

The sky is dark, even at midday. It's freezing. Thick, choking ash covers your house, your street, your town – maybe even your whole country. You've just experienced a supervolcano.

A supervolcano is a super-massive volcanic eruption. There haven't been any in recent history, but we know that they rocked the world in **prehistoric** times.

Yellowstone National Park, USA, lies on the site of a supervolcano. It's not a mountain, but a huge, flat **caldera** with magma bubbling beneath. About 640,000 years ago, it blasted out so much ash and gas that it blocked the Sun and plunged the whole world into winter. Beware – it could erupt again soon.

Volcanic ash can darken the sky and smother plants and crops.

Dino disaster

Some experts think that supervolcanoes helped to wipe out the dinosaurs. Could they wipe out human life, too?

The picture on the right shows what an eruption of the Yellowstone caldera could look like from space.

prehistoric from the time before history was written down

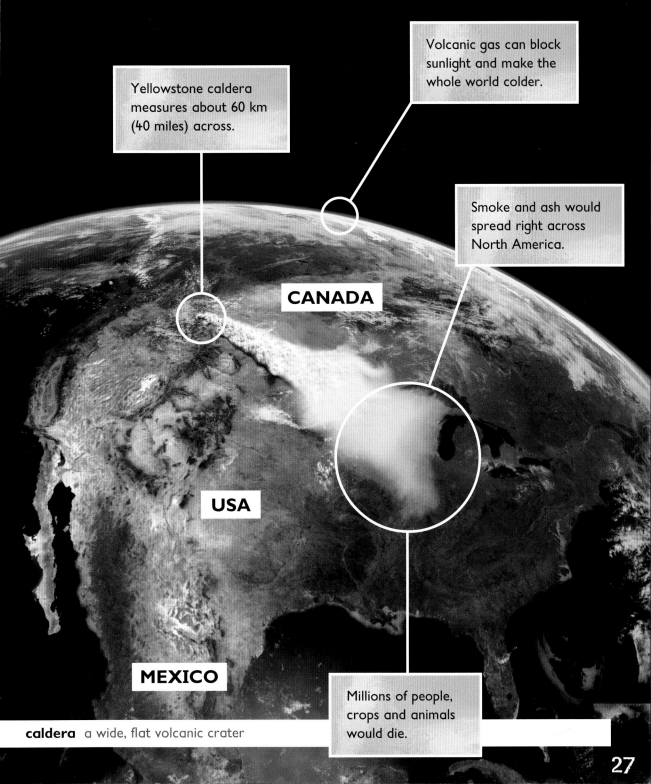

Yellowstone caldera measures about 60 km (40 miles) across.

Volcanic gas can block sunlight and make the whole world colder.

Smoke and ash would spread right across North America.

CANADA

USA

MEXICO

Millions of people, crops and animals would die.

caldera a wide, flat volcanic crater

Are you safe?

So, do you think you can escape if a volcano decides to blow? How are you going to make sure you don't get frazzled?

You can visit active volcanoes in many places around the world. This is the crater of Poas volcano in Costa Rica.

If a volcano goes off near you, there are some things you can do. Firstly, obey instructions! When Mount St Helens erupted in 1980, the area was **evacuated** – but some people refused to leave their homes. That was the end of them.

The picture on the right gives you some more tips on surviving if a volcano blows.

 Avoid valleys: lava and pyroclastic flows will run here.

evacuate to leave an area to avoid danger

Here's Popocatépetl in Mexico blowing its top. If you were standing on it, where would you run?

Extra hazards

Look out for poisonous snakes and insects on the slopes of an erupting volcano. They'll be running for their lives, too.

Avoid snow. It could boil and steam, or melt into deadly mud.

Head for a high ridge or craggy **outcrop**.

Hiding behind a boulder could protect you from flying rocks or splattering lava.

outcrop   an area of bare rock that's raised from the ground

Glossary

breaker a large, white-topped wave that is breaking onto the shore

caldera a wide, flat volcanic crater

crater the bowl-shaped opening of a volcano

crust the layer of hard rock that forms the Earth's surface

erupt to burst out suddenly

evacuate to leave an area to avoid danger

fertile full of things called nutrients, which help crops to grow

fumarole a crack or hole in the ground that gives out steam and gases

geyser a jet of hot water or steam spurting up from the ground

lahar a flow of mud down a volcano

lava flow a trickle or river of lava

lava tube a crust of cooled lava covering a lava flow

magma molten (melted) rock from inside the Earth

outcrop an area of bare rock that's raised from the ground

prehistoric from the time before history was written down

pyroclastic flow a fast-flowing river of hot volcanic ash, rocks and gas

satellite a machine that is sent into space to collect and send back information

sense to detect something using natural senses, such as hearing

spring a place where water flows from the ground

tsunami a giant wave, or series of waves, forming a huge wall of water

vent the tube that leads from inside a volcano to its surface

Further information

Books

Volcanoes! by Anne Schreiber (National Geographic Society, 2008) How volcanoes work and stories of fascinating eruptions, with brilliant photographs.

Into the Volcano: A Volcano Researcher at Work by Donna O'Meara (Kids Can Press, 2007) Follow a real volcanologist as she goes to work visiting volcanoes, making measurements, and studying her results in the lab.

Volcanoes and Earthquakes by Susanna Van Rose (Dorling Kindersley, 2008) An introduction to volcanoes and earthquakes with lots of stunning photos, plus charts and a CD-ROM.

Websites

www.enchantedlearning. com/crafts/nature/ volcano This page shows you how to make a working model of an erupting volcano, using vinegar and baking soda.

http://library.thinkquest. org/17457/english.html A fun-packed volcano site with pictures, facts, games and a database of volcanoes around the world.

www.nationalgeographic. com/ngkids/0312/main. html National Geographic's introduction to volcanoes features exciting animations and videos.

http://vulcan.wr.usgs.gov/ Photo/volcano_cams. html Links to webcams allowing you to view real volcanoes in action.

www.geology.sdsu.edu/ how_volcanoes_work In-depth information on every aspect of volcanoes, with lots of photos and diagrams.

Films

Earth – The Power of the Planet (BBC, 2007) A brilliant BBC series in which Dr Iain Stewart explains the science of volcanoes, earthquakes and more.

Eruption of Mount St Helens directed by George Casey (E-Realbiz. com, 2000) Detailed documentary about the famous real-life volcanic eruption that hit the USA in 1980.

Volcano directed by Mick Jackson (20th Century Fox, 1997) An exciting big-screen movie that explores the impact of a huge volcanic eruption.

Index